Shameka Oliver

SOUL TIES

Recognizing & Overcoming the Ties That Bind

Copyright © 2022 Shameka Oliver

All rights reserved. Printed in the United States of America. No part of this book may be used or reproduced in any manner whatsoever without written permission except in the case of brief quotations in critical articles or reviews.

Cover Design:
Typesetting, Book Layout by
Enger Lanier Taylor for In Due Season Publishing

Published By: In Due Season Publishing ®
Huntsville, Alabama
indueseasonpublishing@gmail.com
www.indueseasonpublishing.com

ISBN-13: 978-1-970057-16-4
ISBN-10: 1-970057-16-5

Shameka Oliver

Dedication

To my mother who always let me be free to be myself and gave me her blessing to tell my story.

To my children. May they live in wisdom and reap the generational blessings of God's covenant promises.

To teenagers and young adults and all readers. May you be delivered by knowledge as you read this book.

Shameka Oliver

Preface

When we go through life insecure or ignorant about our identity and purpose, we tend to carelessly make covenants, also known as soul ties, with people we were never meant to connect with on that level. Some people are meant to stay only for a season. Then there are those who were strategically placed in our path by the enemy to distract, derail, confuse, steal from, or destroy us. Either way, God knows our weaknesses before we confessed them and sent His Son for the redemption of sin and restoration into our proper positions seated in heavenly places in the Kingdom of God.

The thief cometh not, but for to steal, and to kill, and to destroy: I am come that they might have life, and that they might have it more abundantly.
John 10:10

The very first impression on us about the world and ourselves is what we perceive from our family of origin. What they think of the world; what they think of us, and what they feel about their place in the world. And ultimately, what they think of God. We then go through life trying to unlearn all the things that do not align with us and our overall well-being while searching to be filled with those mindsets that do. Strongholds that may appear in our lives or generationally are spirits of rejection, rebellion, lust, orphan spirit, and spirits of shame. Many times, these spirits take root early in those who go on to struggle with soul ties, identity crisis, and toxic relationships.

This is a book about my experiences with soul ties, the open doors or wounds that make way for them to be formed, and the process of healing from ungodly soul ties. There are different types of soul ties and many ranges of side effects of soul ties. My prayer is that as you read this book you be set free and delivered from the stronghold of ungodly soul ties.

Soul ties can be defined as:

> In many cases, it is said to come into existence after two people have been physically intimate. In others, it is said to form after an intensely close spiritual or emotional relationship. Common examples of soul ties refer to those formed with partners from previous relationships. Usually, this person had a vital role in and influence on your life for such a long time that a deep bond or tie was formed. However, that bond may not have necessarily ended when the relationship did.

A spiritual/emotional connection you have to someone after being intimate with them, usually after engaging in sexual intercourse. Even to the point that when you want to move on, you still feel as if they are a part of you and a part of you is with them, causing you to feel unwhole as if you've given up some of yourself intangible that cannot be easily possessed again.

Soul ties can also be formed with demonic spirits from viewing pornography and masturbation because you come into agreement with spirits in the spiritual realm that God did not intend for you to come into contact with. Now you have made an agreement or covenant with this spirit, and it has legal right to operate curses in your life. You will live bound until you gain knowledge and an understanding and come out of agreement with them.

CHAPTER 1

Sin

There are many ways soul ties can be formed. The most common way is through sexual sin such as fornication, masturbation, and pornography. Soul ties can also be formed through occult groups, and other unhealthy relationships that bind a soul together with another's soul: their minds, will, and emotions. The enemy comes in every open door or wound and tries to steal our identity through spirits of lust, shame, rejection, and whatever other way he can come against our true identity. These are the things that drive us to make these ungodly soul ties and entangle ourselves in cycles and cycles of dysfunction. It keeps us from living up to our full potential and who we are called to be in the Kingdom of God. Ungodly soul ties hinder or completely stop the work that needs to be done in the earth according to the perfect will of God. Not only that, but they have access to enslave and wound us mentally, emotionally, physically, and spiritually.

Shameka Oliver

Christ has set us free to live a free life. So, take your stand! Never again let anyone put a harness of slavery on you.
Galatians 5:1

In my fifteen years of being an adult, I see how the spirits of lust, pride, and rebellion ruled my life and made many of my decisions just as the decisions of peers of my generation. We were driven by the influence of the songs we danced and sang along to in the club. "I-N-D-E-P-E-N-D-E-N-T, do you know what that means?" Boosie, Beyonce, Drake, Rihanna, and anything that boosted our egos and declared our freedom and right to rebel or not be controlled as we sang and danced along. We did not quite understand that we were coming into covenant with every word spoken. As I look back, I see how these words that I proclaimed shaped my thought processes pertaining to relationships, goals, and ultimately my expectations in life. At the very young age of 17, I had already developed an independent attitude, and by then, rebellion, lust, and pride were already planted in my spirit.

It was not until I turned 18 and got my first apartment with my cousin as my roommate that I began to live as the adult I thought I was and do what I thought adults did; have sex. Although I had messed around here and there, this was my time to really be independent. As a teenager, I had gone through enough with being so sheltered and constantly fighting my mom and stepfather, mostly because I just wanted to fit in. I didn't realize it at this age, but it was never in God's plan for me to fit in. He set me apart for His will.

I knew you before I formed you in your mother's womb. Before you were born, I set you apart and appointed you as my prophet to the nations.
Jeremiah 1:5

As I was beginning to get comfortable with being an adult and independent thing my freshman year in college, I was struck with a poloidal cyst at the bottom of my tailbone. For days I tried to ignore what seemed to be a simple boil and even attempted to doctor it myself with help. I did anything to avoid interrupting the normal schedule of underage drinking and partying. I remember pleading with God to deliver me when the pain kicked in. I asked God for all kinds of forgiveness. Something about this situation felt like punishment or even a curse. It was the most excruciating pain I had ever been through. I remember my grandmother coming with me to the hospital and I literally screamed as they attempted to remove what they could of the infection, only to determine I needed surgery to completely remove it. Not only that, but the surgery put an end to all my partying, drinking, and adulting for about six long months.

Shameka Oliver

The ties to the lifestyle were so strong that there were times that I did what I wanted to do sooner than I was supposed to. The recovery process was very difficult and very depressing. There was therapy a few times a week, and then finally, the suction pump I carried everywhere with me for the last few weeks. Alas, I can get back to what I thought was adulting properly with no interruptions. I recovered and would never look back on the lesson until years later.

By now, it was my second semester of college and I really needed to be playing catch up due to the previous semester's unexpected occurrence. Instead, I was more focused on hanging out with my friends and having fun. At the time, I was living on campus currently and still barely making it to class. I was so consumed with what was happening around me and so deeply tied into my current friendships that I couldn't see past what I was doing enough to even think about what I was supposed to be focused on. In other words, my priorities were completely upside down. This was a result of the toxic and dysfunctional cycles riding my bloodline. I grew up bound spiritually, mentally, and generationally, meaning there were covenants made knowingly and unknowingly through the bloodline and other influences from media, books, and my peers.

There was no one over my shoulder telling me what I needed to be doing or who I was called to be. I had already decided I was an adult and responsible long before turning 18. I couldn't wait to make my own decisions and be free from the cycles I had seen around me. I recognized the negative cycles but still was not quite mature enough to understand it spiritually. I could hear God and knew Him but still wasn't quite mature enough to understand the realness of His presence and power of His hand. At this age I was so full of rebellion from what I felt was the oppressed and neglected lifestyle I felt I lived growing up. I decided I was never going to live a way contrary to what was comfortable to me. I knew I was going to do something, but I didn't know what or how. I did what I saw in my family, on the movies and on television. I couldn't wait to go to the club and have my first underage drink. It was what I thought it meant to finally be independent.

Going back to all the partying and drinking that clearly wasn't working previously, I found myself suspended from college after my freshman year. I was so lost and confused. I had no clue what I was supposed to do with life. One day while walking to work an army recruiter stopped me. Now if I never said never, I still always knew I would never join the Army in the back of my mind. At this point, I was so desperate for something different that the thought penetrated my stubbornness and I found myself on the way to Basic Training a few months later.

Being away from everything I knew and was comfortable and familiar to me was one of the best things that could have happened at that time in my life. I was so lost and confused that I literally cried out to God to do something and rescue me and then the Army recruiter showed up. God always moved this way for me and would many more times in my life.

When they call on me, I will answer. I will be with them in trouble. I will rescue and honor them.
Psalms 91:15

This time gave me a chance to listen to the voice of Holy Spirit within me. It gave me a chance to define who I was and would be for myself and to overcome the stereotypes and boxes placed before me to fit into. During this time, I realized my best friend in the world was Jesus and witnessed His supernatural power pushing me to complete the task at hand, which was His will and already written for me to complete. When I returned home seven months later, I was stronger spiritually, physically, and mentally. I remember being different. I didn't fit in at all. I was uninterested in all the conversations around me, and it seemed everyone was uninterested in mine. I was still very disciplined for a while. However, with time I was pulled back into the former dysfunctional cycles I had before.

While I was in the second level of training, we had more freedom, and I had gotten back to my regular past time of partying and drinking every chance I got. Once I got home, I was back to the regular revelry. I also found myself in a relationship. While I was on Christmas break from Basic Training, I ran into this guy at the Greyhound bus station who kept staring at me. I sarcastically offered him some candy. He smiled and asked me to come sit with him, and I did. He was already in AIT from the same place as me and on his way home too, so we exchanged numbers. I remember him telling me that I had to call him by a certain day. I didn't realize it then, but after knowing him for a while, he probably had decisions to make.

Consequently, on the way back to training, we ran into each other again. We had only talked maybe once briefly over the break. He had the nerve to ask me to buy him a muffin, so I did. I was just being nice because he asked, and I could. That turned into us hanging out at Greyhound and sitting together on the bus back to Fort Jackson. That is how we fell in love. He sang songs by Chris Brown out loud with his headphones on most of the way and wooed me the rest. When we arrived, it was time to say goodbye. He gave me his address to write him since I was still in basic and couldn't really use the phone, and he would be graduating AIT and leaving soon. When we spoke again, he had finally received my letter while in Korea. I was in

AIT now, and we began to consider ourselves dating. When he came back from Korea, I was there to greet him, and He even put the ring he promised on my hand. Of course, we didn't wait. We were already so in love. This relationship went on for about a year before it ended, with us remaining great friends.

A few months after the breakup, I began dating a guy I knew through mutual friends. We all hung out, got drunk, and did what drunk friends do - laugh, freestyle, revel, and lust. This behavior seemed like tradition by this time. What does **revelry** mean in the Bible; noisy partying or merrymaking?

Neither be ye idolaters, as were some of them; as it is written, The people sat down to eat and drink, and rose up to play. **1 Corinthians 1:7**

Let us behave properly as in the day, not in carousing and drunkenness, not in sexual promiscuity and sensuality, not in strife and jealousy. **Romans 13:13**

Envying, drunkenness, carousing, and things like these, of which I forewarn you, just as I have forewarned you, that those who practice such things will not inherit the kingdom of God. **Galatians 5:21**

Carousing - the activity of drinking alcohol and enjoying oneself with others in a noisy, lively way.

Sensuality - the enjoyment, expression, or pursuit of physical, especially sexual, pleasure.

Chapter 2
Trauma

When you have not dealt with the generational curses operating through your bloodline or dealt with the trauma you will go through life encountering toxic, purposeless, and problematic relationships. Some people who we would consider "players" go through life feeling as though they need multiple people for multiple needs. This is a result of spirits such as pride, vanity, and rebellion. Others may be looking to deeply fill a void left by abandonment, childhood rejection, or mother and father wounds not realizing that each time they attempt to fill that void with anything other than Christ, they open the door a little wider.

Then there are some that just go through life carelessly and ignorant of who they are in the kingdom and are tossed to and fro by every wave. Some people may be so consumed with sexual sin that this is the only thing that they seem to be proud of. We hear this perspective pushed a lot in hip hop music and has cost many to be bound by perversion. Whichever category any of us fall in, the enemy and the plot to destroy your identity and forfeiting your inheritance by forming ungodly soul ties remain the same. It is important for us to recognize the schemes of the enemy. He desires to keep us, and our entire bloodline locked out of our destiny. Once we receive knowledge and insight on the plot against us it is our responsibility to overcome evil and cover others.

Lest Satan should get an advantage of us: for we are not ignorant of his devices. **Hebrews 2:11**

(for the weapons of our warfare are not carnal, but mighty through God to the pulling down of strong holds;) 5casting down imaginations, and every high thing that exalteth itself against the knowledge of God and bringing into captivity every thought to the obedience of Christ. **2 Corinthians 10:4-5**

For our struggle is not against flesh and blood, but against the rulers, against the authorities, against the powers of this dark world and against the spiritual forces of evil in the heavenly realms. **Ephesians 6:12**

Rejection is one of the doors the enemy can use to gain access into your life. It can begin as early as in the womb for many different reasons. The mother carrying the child may not want the baby for her own selfish reasons or she may be dealing with rejection herself or other toxic situations that would cause her to reject her baby in the womb. Whatever the circumstances may be surrounding the rejection it can be felt by the growing baby. This is called prenatal rejection. A lot of people go through life never realizing that they have been suffering from rejection since the womb. You can also develop a rejected mindset from father wounds as well as rejection from siblings, other family members, friends, peers, or other social groups. These types of wounds will cause you to go through life feeling less than who you truly are and not walking in the fullness of who The Great I AM created you to be. This is not the will of the Father concerning your life.

Beloved, I wish above all things that thou mayest prosper and be in health, even as thy soul prospereth.
3 John 2:2

A person can deal with rejection due to abandonment from one or both parents. In my case, my father was in California, and I was in Louisiana for most of my life. While I was growing up, there were times I went months without hearing from or talking to him. I remember him providing here and there as a child and living his day-to-day life with my little brother, his mom, and two brothers. Although I knew my father loved me greatly, these were the conditions of our relationship as a child. For some people, this is a normal cycle of life, but this is not God's original design. I did not realize how much this affected me until I went through deliverance from mother and father wounds. I was always very skilled at suppressing my true feelings, so it's no wonder I carried these wounds around for so long. I felt abandonment and rejection from an early age which caused me to go through life with insecurities and resentment, which manifested as fear and rebellion, and other unclean spirits. The nature of a mother is to nurture, comfort, and teach as Holy Spirit is unto us. Mother wounds manifest as a lack of confidence, lack of trust, difficulty setting boundaries, feeling ignored, and poor self-image. The nature of a father is to physically provide, and give identity, and security, just like our heavenly Father. Father wounds manifest as a lack of security in your identity, double-mindedness, independence, fear, and a hard time submitting to men.

For my father and my mother have forsaken me,
but the LORD will take me in.
Psalm 27:10

A few months after my brief engagement (here I was in lust this time) because that is what our relationship was founded on. We tried to make the most out of it. It was cute at first until it wasn't. The lust turned into entitlement, and I began to see red flags telling me this person may be abusive. After an incident or two or THREE, I finally decided this was not what I wanted for my life. I didn't want to live in sin at all. I wanted to live free from sexual sin and go deeper with God. At that time, I was in the Army Reserves, in college full-time, and working. I had a car and a roommate. Things were perfect. I began the process of going on military orders to pursue my nursing license, funded fully by the military while getting paid. I couldn't wait to leave and do something more with my life.

In some situations, due to the forming of an ungodly soul tie, one or both persons involved may feel entitled, or let's just say the spirit of entitlement creeps its way into the relationship. For example, a person may feel as though you are entitled to perform certain sexual favors for them whenever they want and will get upset or make you feel bad if you don't. Another example is when a person feels as though they should be receiving more of your time or feel as though they should be prioritized above other people or things.

What does entitlement mentality mean?

The entitlement mentality is defined as a sense of deservingness or being owed a favor when little or nothing has been done to deserve special treatment. It's the "you owe me" attitude. Entitlement is a narcissistic personality trait.

This usually sets in immediately after pre-marital sex but can also appear in marital sex when the covenant was formed on ungodly ties. Entitlement is what would cause a person to stalk, harass, or be angered when you do not do what it is they desire. Entitlement is a direct open door to the spirit of Jezebel, which opens the door to many other strongholds ushered in by sexual sin. Entitlement can also be an issue in ungodly soul ties formed other ways other than sex, such as spending a lot of time having intimate conversations with another person or ungodly soul ties formed from trauma bonding or formed upon other ungodly structures or principles. A lot of times we form ungodly soul ties in hope that something will change, and God would bless the covenant we made in ignorance. One thing I have learned is God is a God of order, and it is important to follow carefully godly principles and pay attention to His way of doing things. It will cost you more, in the end, to do things contrary to His will.

For the wages of sin is death; but the gift of God is eternal life through Jesus Christ our Lord.
Romans 6:23

Trauma bonding is another way soul ties can be formed. When two people suffer from the same type of unhealed trauma or share similar unhealed wounds they may bond based off these facts. This can be a very toxic way to form a relationship, especially when it leads to an immediate sexual relationship. In these relationships you feel more deeply damaged and betrayed when the other person does something that causes your entitlement to be threatened. Entitlement in toxic relationships and ungodly soul ties can end in one person hurting the other or both hurting each other mentally, emotionally, spiritually, physically, and even at times, fatally. An entitled person may seek to harm you or your reputation when they feel they have been treated below what they feel entitled. The results of this range from slut shaming, defamation, harassment, black balling, and other various ways a person may take out their anger or jealousy because of the wound.

- According to Medical News Today, "Trauma bonding is a psychological response to abuse. It occurs when the abused person forms an unhealthy bond with the person who abuses them."

- According to healthline.com This emotional attachment, known as a trauma bond, develops out of a repeated cycle of abuse, devaluation, and positive reinforcement.

Trauma bonds are emotional bonds with an individual that arise from a recurring, cyclical pattern of abuse perpetuated by intermittent reinforcement through rewards and punishments (Wikipedia).

Turns out the guy from the Greyhound ended up becoming a great friend over time. He had been deployed, and we talked as friends regularly. One day I logged into social media and could hardly understand what I was seeing. His mother had passed away. It was unexpected. She and I had a good relationship and kept in touch. I knew how close he and his family were and how devastating this would be, so I agreed to visit when he returned to post. I went to visit in August, and I came home pregnant.

The moment I saw the positive results I felt like my life was over and so were my future plans. I had to go to drill and tell my leaders I was no longer eligible for orders due to my pregnancy. Shame set in so heavily that I went from praying and communing with God all day every day, to not at all. This went on for most of my pregnancy until one day, it was my 23rd birthday, I went to church, and something broke. From that day forward, I began moving toward my future again. I had been in such a depressed state. Not only was I pregnant with my first child out of wedlock, but so was my baby sister. This was a very hard pill to swallow because I thought I had at least given a very good example of how to not get pregnant at 16. There was a spiritual war raging in our bloodline, and I was beginning to get angry about it.

When I had my son, I remember feeling so many emotions. Especially once we got home and it was just the two of us. After sharing that I was pregnant, I was informed by a family member that he had another baby on the way as well. I was devastated and in disbelief. This was the girl he had told me about. I didn't know things were even that serious. I thought, "This can't be real right now. I can't possibly be having his baby." You know what, there was that one night over the summer. I mean we didn't go that far, but maybe it's his. These were the immediate thoughts the spirit of shame planted in my heart. I began to feed the idea that someone else could have fathered my child even while knowing by way of facts that was not likely or possible. The seed began to grow until I looked at my son one day and knew without a doubt who I made him with, and it stopped. We took a paternity test, and I can honestly say he has never stopped providing for his son since. Because of the circumstances of my pregnancy, my son's father and I didn't have the best relationship. I knew. He knew. And when I held my son for the first time, I saw his face but because of the circumstances of the covenant I had made with this man, so many ungodly spirits were free to come in and plant their plots from hell, in an attempt to derail my son's destiny. During the first six months of my son's life, I was either high or drunk, and on top of that, entangled in some type of drama with my current toxic situation.

That situation began with a summer fling pre-pregnancy and ended after a few domestic situations, which caused me to fear for my life and even my baby's life. It wasn't hard to walk away, but it was hard to let go. That soul tie was drenched in the demonic. I remember knowing I was in a situation that didn't feel real. It was like I could see outside myself. I was so broken and alone. I just wanted my chance to be dumb like everybody else. I remember saying that. He would take my car, money, do whatever he wanted, and I just let him. I remember the day the atmosphere broke when I began to play, "Shake Us Again" by Juanita Bynum. From that day, something shook me, and I never found myself in that type of darkness ever again.

Soul ties can take us down paths that were never meant for us. Some lead to permanent destruction and loss. Thankfully by God's grace I was never too far gone to realize all I had to do was turn away from my sin and draw near to God.

Draw nigh to God, and he will draw nigh to you. Cleanse your hands, ye sinners; and purify your hearts, ye double minded.
James 4:8

My life quickly began to take a turn for the good when I finally let that situation go. I had allowed myself to be bound to false responsibilities of another person. I was ready to focus on me and my son now. I began working overnight at a hotel and befriended the security guard. This man began to teach me deep spiritual and biblical things that I had never heard of in Church. I began to witness different manifestations of signs, wonders, and miracles. As these things began to happen and I began to walk deeper with God, I would hear Him say to me regularly, "Do you see me now?" It was so real and happened so often that I began to shake in the fear of the Lord each time it would occur.

Blessed are the pure in heart: for they shall see God.
Matthew 5:8

Chapter 3

Identity Crisis

This same year, I learned a lesson that would follow me years later. Whenever there is an encounter with God, always expect a test or demonic attack to follow. After a few months on my new journey, I found myself in love again. It was summer training in the Reserves, and I found myself attracted to this guy. I remember the day we met I was under my covers on my bunk mourning the loss of my nephew, and I decided to get up and go work out. I was going to hang out that day to get my mind off my grief. That night is when we first met. As we began to talk, I discovered that he had lost his mother less than a year ago. We were there for two weeks, so we began to hang out and converse a lot. These talks led to us staying connected and him coming to visit me. He was from North Louisiana and a College student at the time. Things got intimate as soon as we were able, and the relationship continued from there. He went back to school, and of course, that's when the entitlement, jealousy, and insecurity kicked in. We were so in lusty love that he could hardly maintain and focus on all that he needed to focus on in school including dealing with his own grief. I was so consumed with my love for him that when things didn't go my way I remember crying randomly for days. I was so in love, and I just wanted him. Whatever the cost, I knew we had to be together. He would come back and forth to appease me, and I would make sure to give him something to remember. Not realizing that memory would only last so long until he was back at school in a different environment and doing whatever he felt he needed to do.

At the end of the semester, he finally decided to move in with my son and me. Neither one of us were working or in a stable situation, but we were so in love, and that's all that mattered for months. We maintained until we both eventually started working at the same casino. All of this happened in a matter of eight months. We met and started to build a life together. He knew that I wanted to be married, so after a few incidents, he proposed. I was happy, but I knew he did it just to please me. Maybe I was somewhat ready to be a wife, but, we were both much further from the mark than I knew. I couldn't see past what I wanted at the time. We eventually settled on a date and began to make preparations.

The preparation in itself was a lot to go through. It began to highlight mother and father wounds that I was accustomed to ignoring. I went through so many emotions about whether I wanted my father to walk me down the aisle and why. So many buried emotions came up pertaining to wounds that I had been covering up and ignoring. Shame was having its way with me again. I remember feeling ashamed of where I came from and my parents. When I looked at my soon to be husband's family background it looked nothing like mine. His parents were pastors, and so were many others in his family. He and his siblings were raised in the church, and the church life is all they knew.

Meanwhile, I come from a family with a history of gang bangers, pimps, and drug dealers. It wasn't until my father and uncle came, and we all got together days before the wedding, and they shared stories with us that I began to understand my father more and was able to begin forgiving him. At this point, I didn't even realize how much resentment I held toward him. It was a huge relief, and he is such a naturally lovable person, so everyone loved him, and everything went well.

If your brother sins, rebuke him, and if he repents, forgive him. **Luke 17:3**

Blessed are the merciful, for they shall receive mercy. **Matthew 5:7**

A new commandment I give to you, that you love one another: just as I have loved you, you also are to love one another. **John 13:34**

Although I had finally begun to recognize my mother and father wounds, I still was not ready to face them completely. I'd rather mind my current happiness. That was more important to me. I married the man I was in love with, in spite of the history of our relationship. Our union was immediately met with what seemed to be the demonic realm. I spent two long nights in jail due to false accusations after a traffic stop and then proceeded to our honeymoon in Florida. I remember the feeling of shame. It felt dirty, nasty, and funky. I tried my best to enjoy my honeymoon despite how ashamed I felt and carried the shame along home for a while when we left. This was the way my marriage began.

We returned home to our two-bedroom apartment and got back to life as we knew it. The relationship had already been tapping into the more toxic side, and entitlement had long before already been established. I can't say it wasn't on both ends, but let's just say one of us was much, much more entitled than the other. So much so, that being intimate had more than likely been an issue for some time. In the beginning of our relationship, we were so in lust that all we wanted to do was be intimate. As time went on and different things wounded the relationship being intimate became a thing of entitlement. It became more and more unappealing. Between the two of us, lust, perversion, shame, rejection, and rebellion began to manifest as insecurities, control, and even paranoia.

We then began to have issues about intimacy. Naturally, we had two different views on what that meant. By the time I had my daughter, we had been married a little over a year, and I was working on myself as a wife. In other words, I was making sure to pay attention to my wifely duties. Hubby and I had just had our first child together, and we were still in newlywed bliss. At least, that is what I thought until Valentine's Day of the next year. We had exchanged gifts, and I was on my way to the nail shop.

Contrary to what I would have usually done, I opened his Facebook messenger on the phone he had left in the car. He had been excited to play his new PlayStation. What I saw was the last message of an obviously deleted thread. I confronted him, and it ended with me returning the PlayStation -and him leaving. He eventually came home, but things would never be the same from that point.

We proceeded with life as usual. I tried my best to be an excellent wife to my husband, and we continued in the same displeasing cycles of not caring for each other and tearing each other down. In March of that year, my great aunt Glo went on to be with the Lord. The entire family flew from Louisiana on the same flight to San Diego. This was a matriarch in our family and to a lot of OG gangsters. Her funeral seemed like something off a movie. There were gangsters from different neighborhoods everywhere. Then there was the only OG blood there, who was my dad. Everyone knew my earthly father as Gangster Rabb, but to me, he was just my dad. He was rolling in his 1970 Chevy Caprice that he had recently decked out. I always felt a bit annoyed when he would look at me crazy, explaining why I could not "roll with him" when I asked. He would literally laugh in my face when I asked to accompany him this same visit. I didn't understand it then, but it would all make sense later.

Jesus replied, "You do not realize now what I am doing, but later you will understand."
John 13:7

While on the trip, Hubby and I did our usual bickering and disagreeing. My uncle and cousin even called themselves defending him against my sarcastic and smart-mouthed abuse. As a result, we ended the trip without me ever knowing about the scenarios of paranoia going through my troubled husband's head the entire trip. Had I gone to be with someone else? Was I planning on getting him jumped? These were the kind of things that came up once we arrived home.

Two months later, I received a call as I was settling in from work. My aunt called to tell me that my dad had been shot, but he was okay. I remember making a few light jokes, but I immediately got on my knees to pray after hanging up. Minutes to hours later, I received a call from my cousin, who had been with my dad every day, saying that he was dead. All I could do was ask questions. Who told you that? How do you know? Who else said it? I was not ready to accept such a fact. I stayed up the remainder of the night looking at the walls and contemplating that it was a lie. Maybe when the sun came up, things would be different. Unfortunately, when the sun came up, that wasn't the case. The fact began to settle in that my dad was dead. We had just recently started to have a much closer relationship, and just like that, he wasn't coming back. On top of losing my father unexpectedly and in such an odd situation, he had left possessions that would cause discord and strife in the family.

I went back and forth to San Diego a few times to help settle my dad's affairs which really ended up being a great revelation of everything my dad said to me without speaking. All the pieces to the puzzle finally made sense with every person in their proper place. Now I realized what all the crazy comments and long stares in the eyes meant. How shielded I had been. I was

27 years old and had never felt as unsafe as I did, knowing that my dad was no longer on this earth. He had practically hidden an entire reality from me my entire life, and everyone aided him in doing so.

By the time I got home from San Diego, I had lost enough weight to be very noticeable. Not only was I fighting my husband the entire time, but I was also fighting my family over my dad's arrangements. It was so bad that I could literally "hear" my dad fussing for me, even attending the funeral services after all the drama/trauma I had been through. I found peace in staying home and letting my aunt attend in my absence.

You would think that losing my father would have brought my husband and me together, but it was the complete opposite in our situation. After the summer, I mentioned to my aunt that Hubby and I were looking to join a church. I had a deep relationship with God and didn't feel I needed church at the time, but he grew up as a Baptist preacher's kid and felt we should join one. She would send us an address a few weeks later.

When I first visited the church, I remember it being an amazing and exciting praise and worship service. I felt so much freedom I ended up joining without my husband present. He was away at drill. When he returned and visited, he joined as well. When I looked back, I began to see how out of order this new journey began. We quickly became faithful members and tithers. Things were going well at church but unstable in our relationship. We were constantly still arguing. Things were very intense around this time in the spiritual realm. There was so much going on all at one time, and I was wearing many hats every day while managing not to deal with any of my recent trauma.

For God is not the author of confusion, but of peace, as in all churches of the saints.
1 Corinthians 14:33

Things got so bad at home that I decided I needed to take a break around the corner at my grandparents, which was temporary in an attempt to save my marriage. My spouse did not comprehend my pure intentions and wisdom in my thought process. At that time, I had found out on the rare occasion we had been intimate while separated that I was pregnant. Our marriage was still problematic, and the stress caused me to miscarry at nine weeks. After a couple of months of separation my husband was laid off from his construction job and decided he was moving back to North Louisiana. We had already signed and had my name removed from the lease weeks before.

After two months of living with my grandparents and recovering from a miscarriage, I found an available apartment in the same location I had lived when I met

Hubby. My kids and I got comfortable and began to get our new life on track. We were still attending the church, and I was not sure what people thought of my husband's absence. I only assumed that they thought he was on military leave or working. Either way, no one ever really asked. I began to adjust to being a single mother of two, and before long, Hubby and I began to converse again. After getting what I believe was confirmation that this was the way things would continue to be, I made the decision to be the wife I was influenced to be and take my husband back and make it work. I thought that it was easier this way.

We were separated again by the summer. It was so bad that we had planned a trip around July 4th that I would go on without him. I remember feeling free. I enjoyed this temporary freedom a couple months only to make the decision to make it work again. By this time, Hubby had become a truck driver. He was acting differently now. He would get mad and accuse me of being this and that, doing whatever with everyone. By this time, I had looked in the mirror and worked on myself so much that I began to give no reaction.

It was New Year's Eve weekend, and we were engaged in the usual dysfunctional routine and coping mechanisms we were used to before a church service. We went to church all night only to do the usual and pretend nothing ever happened. This was the toxic cycle my marriage had come down to. By now, I had truly had enough. I couldn't make sense of God wanting this type of relationship for me. I began to conclude that this was my will and not God's perfect will for my life. No matter what I tried it just didn't work. I felt that just because we want something, and we get it doesn't mean God has to bless it. This was my logic surrounding my current situation.

We had moved up in influence in the church very quickly. Now that I look back, maybe instantly. During one of our brief separations, I was invited to attend a training class at the church. By the end of the process and my graduation/ordination came, he was back in the picture. The class was very intense, yet natural to me. It stretched me and showed me my potential. At the time of the ordination, I was ordained as a prophetic intercessor. By surprise, I was also ordained as the church administrator. I didn't understand what that meant entirely until I was shown my office after service. My mother, whom I had invited to the church, was ordained as well as an elder. We did not see it then, but the hype that was created by the amount of influence we had was being preyed upon. It was something marketable, new, and fresh to the movement that was already established. They would eventually realize they didn't want what came along with that influence.

If it does evil in My sight by not obeying My voice, then I will think better of the good with which I had Promised to bless it.

Shameka Oliver
Jeremiah 18:10

I stayed quiet long enough to get through the next month and the very first incident following was enough for me. When I noticed my kids, who were six and two at the time, were sitting up in their room watching TV like nothing was happening, I knew it was over. I was not going to raise dysfunctional children who thought this type of behavior was normal. I told him to leave and that was how our relationship officially ended. I kept the ship afloat by any means necessary, which meant me working four part-time jobs as a realtor, cocktail waitress, part-time buffet server, and on-call banquet server. Additionally, I was still the active administrator at the church.

Now I found myself carrying many different loads alone. I was so at the end of living the dysfunctional way I had been living that I weighed the cost and still decided to disconnect from my then husband. From my perspective I spent years trying to be an above average wife, mother, and Christian. I went through so many layers of pain for the next couple of months and faced some of my biggest demons as I began to heal and find myself again. I had put my whole life in a box and the hands of this man that I called my husband.

Who was I anyway besides now another single mother? The spirit of shame began to creep in like never before. It began to manifest as lust, rebellion, and pride. I spent a few months after my separation battling these spirits. I wanted more than anything to erase what I had done. I wanted to divorce as quickly as possible and separate myself from the stronghold of this person with whom I had come into covenant. I just wanted to be free, so even after he refused to sign the divorce papers, I made sure it was official.

And he said, "I heard the sound of you in the garden, and I was afraid, because I was naked, and I hid myself."
Genesis 3:10

Shameka Oliver

When u died

When you died, I didn't cry
I sat up for hours contemplating a lie...
I told myself not yet, we still don't know if he's okay
knowing somewhere in reality I'd have to face it one day

When you died, I didn't cry
I wasn't ready to ask God why
Instead, it was "who told you that" and ignored calls
My phone was going off like crazy, me spending the night staring at the pitch-black walls

When you died I didn't cry
I had to make sense of this horrible dream
Why is everyone in on the cruel joke?
Even the ones I thought were on our team

When you died, I didn't cry
Almost, but not yet
Too soon, I have to shake back
So much to do, no time for tears, grabbed my suitcase it's time to pack

When you died, I didn't cry
if what they said was true...
you were already gone and not coming back...

hid my tears, tucked away my fears, because my biggest bodyguard was you

When you died, I didn't cry
I knew that time would arrive soon
Even then, hidden tears, tucked away fears, i moved on like u wanted me to ..
I heard your voice, how proud you were, keep going, don't give in, keep doing what you do

When you died, I didn't cry
That's not what you told me to do
So, when I finished, I remembered who you were to me, what you would say
I picked myself up, got myself together, and you were that much closer to my life since that day

When you died, I didn't cry…

In Loving Memory of
Kevin Earl "Gangsta Rabb" Spelmon Sr.
Tuesday, May 2, 2017

Chapter 4

Shame

May 1 was my official divorce date. Exactly two years from the day my dad was murdered. I remember the type of feelings that came over me when I received those dates in the mail. I felt anger, pain, shame, bitterness, and then…acceptance. It had been three months since the husband, and I had separated, and what a sickening rollercoaster it had been. Although I weighed the cost of a divorce there was still only so much preparation one's soul can make for this type of severance. Not only had I left my job of three years, but since separation, things had gotten tough at the church. I had begun noticing the lack of concern for what I was going through personally. Yet there were such high expectations for me to fulfill. Finally, it came out at an administrative meeting. I confessed that this was not my primary concern and that I should step down as administrator. The meeting ended with me remaining the acting administrator and motivating myself to do better in my ministry role. Unfortunately, this attempt would lead to another meeting telling me I would no longer be the administrator. I felt disrespected, which led me to retrieve my personal computer, sending a text, and not returning.

Once my divorce was final, I felt I needed to celebrate my freedom by having a divorce party. I had been planning it in the back of my mind, but when it came down to it, I ended up at a local club and strip club with a random friend and her underage cousin. I hadn't been in a club in so long so it was exciting to see so many people I hadn't seen in years. So many people thought I had moved away because they never saw me out and about anymore. I drank and smoked and danced all night. I really let loose. I even cheered on the strippers and tipped them, all while not caring who saw or what they thought. I was celebrating my freedom from the chains I had been in the last few years.

This night out would result in me receiving a Facebook message from someone who had seen me on his way out that night and had messaged me in previous years despite my failure to respond. He would go down in history as the first guy that got my attention and a response via social media. After that, we began to hang out casually and build a friendship with many boundaries.

Not only was I severing a soul tie and divorcing half of our household income and household help in general, but things were slowly beginning to crumble around me as well. This was a life I wasn't used to; being a single mother of two. The quick transition from married and the seemingly most beautiful family to divorced and single with two kids happened in a matter of four months. This rollercoaster ride was traumatic and left new wounds that would need to be dealt with on top of older wounds. I began to struggle financially and at home because of my emotions.

I had tried to cover up and ignore the dysfunction in my bloodline. I was so busy building something that looked a certain way to cover the more accurate picture. I came from a dysfunctional bloodline. One day I began to look around me, so I joined the Army Reserves. I knew I would not be a product of what was represented around me from that point on.

Here I was ten years later, newly divorced, single with two kids, and struggling financially, mentally, and emotionally. My support system began to crumble all at the same time. That same year I would fall out with my best friend of many years. We would later reconcile. Due to my financial instability me and my kids moved into my grandparent's home again. This time my mother was living there, and our communication was not great. This led to constant strife at home. I knew to keep a roof over my head, I had to humble myself, which I did. However, that seemed to provoke more issues. I was just trying to focus on my goals, listen to affirmations and meditation music, and better myself. They must've all thought I was crazy.

By this time, my new friend and I had begun to become intimate yet maintained somewhat strict boundaries. Although I did not understand at the time and did not want to set boundaries, he understood I had just been divorced and I needed time to heal from the relationship and rediscover myself. Although we set boundaries, or should I say he did, he never disrespected me or made me feel I needed to worry about him making me look crazy. He felt neither one of us was ready for a relationship, and although he was 100% correct, I challenged him on it every chance I got. I was eager to have the level of intimacy I was used to, but he was strong enough to stand on what he believed and nothing I could have said or done would change his belief. Our friendship was so natural, and the respect was almost unbelievable to even when I didn't get what I wanted, our relationship continued to go on.

I was still actively pursuing real estate, whatever that meant at the time, and began working another job as a property manager. This job was paying more than I had made in the past and was double the responsibility. Perhaps the pay grade should have been all I needed to know how to do the job properly, but that wasn't the case. From the beginning to the end, the management gave me hell at work. Unfortunately, I called them the "gross sisters" only because they had such bad fruit. I had never witnessed so much drama, mess, and pettiness in the workplace. I was beginning to think it was time to get away from the entire state. They weren't even from the same city, and they were just as wicked as the people I encountered in my social spaces locally.

Upon being presented with an ultimatum I ended up making the decision to resign from the job over switching my real estate license to their broker. I wasn't making any money, only spending on my real estate license, and my job was my only source of income, yet I still chose my mental stability, which was beginning to wear thin, over my income.

I had started attending church again since leaving the summer before. When I returned, I began to slowly focus less on my own goals and more on others and how I could help. This was when I started to get pulled back in. When I left previously after my divorce, there was an incident between the female pastor and me.

When I found myself on the other side of the line, being bullied by a narcissist and her crew, I realized that I needed to step back before things got out of hand. Unfortunately, I still was unaware at the time that I was being challenged by the spirit of Jezebel and her followers. As a result, I went through several spiritual attacks before finally ending my attendance altogether.

When I did this, I immediately began to feel relief. I had been getting bits and pieces of knowledge about prophetic witchcraft, and the more knowledge I gained, the more I began to awake from the spell I had been under and got free. However, there was still a constant mental and spiritual battle that I had never faced before. I was in such a dark place of confusion. I began to hear thoughts in my head that I would automatically know were Satan. He would tell me how I could make things easier, but I knew in my spirit if I could just keep trusting God, He would rescue me.

At this low point in my life, a friend sent me a Facebook live video of a lady talking about catastrophic warfare. Her name was Sophia Ruffin. I had never heard of her before, but her delivery and everything about the word she delivered seemed so accurate. I received the Word and then went on about my regular day-to-day activities. The next video would be of another well-known female prophet sharing her testimony of overcoming ministry trauma about the same spirits as my experience. This opened my eyes and completely woke me to what I had witnessed over the last three years. This realization of this demonic occurrence in God's churches affected me deeply. I would be taking a trip to San Diego for a celebration for my dad's 50th birthday. This would be my first time in San Diego since his passing. I knew I would be changed when I returned, and I made sure to declare this aloud several times.

As soon as I crossed the Louisiana state line on the way home from Texas, I remember a State Trooper swooping quickly onto the interstate, and my stomach instantly felt sick. From that moment, I knew I had to leave Louisiana. I couldn't tolerate it anymore and had to get away.

When I got home, I did not expect the eviction notice. The apartment was managed by the company I had just resigned from, so it was only a matter of time before this day came. They knew the apartment was not in my name, and I witnessed how the previous manager was treated and forced to vacate upon her termination. I didn't have enough in me to care. I just began to pack, not knowing where I was going.

At this time, all that I had been through began to weigh on me so heavily that I began to think I was really about to lose my mind. I began to convince myself I could not check into a local mental home and that I had to do something before I ended up there. Everyone around me must have thought I had it all together because no one could tell or acknowledge how close to the edge I was. I remember constant questions about where I would put my things or what to do as I moved all of my stuff to my grandparent's house. My reply was simply I don't know. I had no clue what I would do, only what I would not do.

Money was tight, so I had begun to hold on to all of my bill money. After selling a few items, I decided to have a garage sale. After all, I had nowhere to keep all of my things anyway. By this time, a comment my son's dad made had settled in my mind, and I was determined to get my son to his dad until I could get a hold of my life. He had suggested we come to where he lived in North Carolina and then later changed his mind. It was too late because I had no other options. I could not imagine moving me, my then 7-year-old son, and 3-year-old daughter into my grandparent's already overcrowded home or anyone else's, for that matter.

Before I could catch my head, I had set a date to leave and had everything planned as far as the trip would go. The plan was that I would fit what I could in my car and get new tires. I stuck to my plan and took the fourteen-plus hour drive alone with my two children from Louisiana to North Carolina. When we arrived at my son's dad's home, it was only their second in person meeting. He had always been a provider but always made excuses as to why he couldn't be present. Luckily, they had kept up through Facetime, and things weren't too awkward.

Of course, I knew things wouldn't go smoothly with my son's dad and me because he had already tried to convince me not to come. I needed him to step in and be an active parent. There was no other option. After much confusion, we drove 1.5 hours to my dear cousin's mom's house, and she agreed to let me stay until I could figure out what I would do. This act of kindness is something that I will forever be grateful for. It changed the trajectory of my life forever. What else would I have ever done? I would drive my son back to his dad the following Monday and register him for school.

It didn't dawn on me until a few days later, but CATASTROPHIC WARFARE had come to take me out and failed. But instead, God answered my prayer and rescued me. I couldn't believe I had made that drive alone in such a short time. It had felt like an out of body experience, but I know without a doubt that the Spirit of God was with me. It had to be God because I was completely out of myself, but now I could feel myself coming back to me.

Shameka Oliver

I Can Feel the Pressure

I can feel the pressure
The walls closing in on me
The light is getting dimmer
I can't think and can hardly see
No one hears my cry for help
If they do, they don't care because it's me
And before the light goes completely out, a door is opened, and I am set free
Free as free can be
No stress, no negativity, just me and the savior that rescued me
Finally sweet relief
Is this real?
Am I dreaming?
This is not at all what I thought it would be
But I remember your word
Your promises
Your love
And accept that what is to be will always be
I can feel the pressure
It is making a diamond out of me

Chapter 5

Grace

By my second week in North Carolina, I had already gotten a job doing night audits at a hotel, which made sense because I still had my daughter at the time, and I figured my cousin could watch her while I worked. This situation continued for a month until, one day, I confronted God. I told Him that I knew He didn't bring me this far to be in a position where the need for help from others binds me. I wrote in my journal about my choice of fathers for my children. The very next day, my ex-hubby called while I was at work. I could tell he was nervous, but I was happy and sad when he suggested it was his turn to have his daughter and that he would be coming to get her before Thanksgiving. I remember her being so happy she began to pack all of her things in a pillowcase. Although this was hard to accept, I knew it was for the best. I thought that I would use this time to get more stable and in a better situation regarding child care.

This was the first time I could remember feeling as though I didn't have to carry a heavy load and only had to focus on my survival. I felt blessed as a mother sending my most prized possessions to live with their fathers and not feeling a bit of uncertainty, only relief and gratitude. I used this time to tune in with myself and heal from the inside out.

While I was working at my night audit job looking up discernment on YouTube, I stumbled upon a well-known inner healing ministry. Her videos were all very intriguing to me, and she shared a lot of information. After watching several videos, I heard her say she was the pastor of a church right there in the area. I could hardly believe it happened that way, but it had. I went to visit the church twice. I remember feeling God so strongly that I was fighting myself not to make a Holy Ghost scene. It had been a while since I had been to church, let alone experienced this level of anointing that was in that place.

After checking the church and pastors out, I was so desperate for deliverance that I messaged her on Facebook, and she directed me to her online mentorship program. I will always consider her somewhat of a spiritual parent to me for the levels of deliverance I received from being a part of the Destiny Training

Academy. During her training is where I began to understand the mother and father wounds that were still affecting me as an adult. I began to understand why I act and respond the way I do and faced the demons I had been ignoring. This process looked like me wanting so badly to fill a void that I checked out for a few months and didn't recognize myself until I returned. The spirit of rebellion and lust came to the surface and tried to have its way in my life. I remember snapping out of it one day, and when I looked back, I realized it was because of the deliverance I was going through that I was getting free from demons that didn't want to go without a fight. It was good to be back to reality and not dancing with the devil, and I could finally focus again!

It was now 2020, and I was working two jobs and getting my mind back to a mentally healthy place. Both of my children were still with their fathers. We had been living in our apartment for a couple of months, and I had recently gotten a more affordable vehicle. Things were going well, and I was in a content place finally with my current relationship status. My male friend and I continued our relationship until I moved, but out of bitterness for his lack of ability to do what I wanted, we stopped talking for a short time. In reality, I knew that he had always been honest with me about his viewpoints on our relationship. He had never once disrespected me, even through my immature and sometimes bitter episodes. I had learned a lot from him about myself, and even though I wasn't ready to admit it, I had grown because of the boundaries he had set in place. I still wanted my way but couldn't resist how he respected me, so our friendship continued, and he even came to visit before the new year began.

His birthday was coming up, and we planned a trip to a Lakers basketball game in New Orleans. Before departing, I spent a day in Louisiana for the first time since I had moved to North Carolina. My ex-hubby and I had agreed that I would get my daughter while I was in Louisiana and that she would then go back with him. I was just getting comfortable with moving freely, and I was not ready to figure out how I would be able to manage with my kids in a new state yet. I had also brought my son with me to stay in Louisiana and return to school because his father would be deploying, and I was very skeptical about sending him to yet another new school in such a short time. The plan was that he would stay with my mother and attend school for the remainder of the year in Louisiana.

When I returned to North Carolina, I was just beginning to get into my routine when the Covid 19 pandemic began. I was at one of my local friend's houses, and we were watching the news, and it seemed as though the zombie apocalypse was going on around the world. I had previously watched the news from work, but I didn't have this feeling. So, I rushed home and immediately began to make plans to get to my kids in Louisiana. My daughter had gone back with her dad, and my son was with my mom. As soon as I realized this pandemic's seriousness, my second job shut down completely. I then let my manager at the hotel know I had to be off to get my kids, and they informed me to file unemployment.

When I went back to North Carolina, my daughter returned with me. By this time, schools had shut down, and we were expecting them to reopen, so my son stayed. After about a month into the pandemic, I realized that things might be shut down for a while, so I sent for my son. My friend would fly with him and come visit again. So, after months, we were together again at our apartment with my cousin as our beloved roomie.

Summer 2020 was the most memorable summer my kids, and I had experienced. In 2020 I drove over 40k miles on my 09 Kia and never hit 100k. So, while the entire world was in a pandemic, we lived our best life ever. I'm sure many people will have the same testimony because this was much needed time spent with loved ones.

Although the pandemic seemed to be a tragic event for most of the world, this was one of the best times of my life. My kids, my cousin (roommate), and I were already used to being homebodies, so now we just felt freer than ever because there was no pressure about being social.

We were fully taking advantage of this time and reflecting on the hidden blessings behind what was happening. I realized this was more than just a pandemic when I found out Morris Cerullo had died. At that moment, I knew it was time for the body of Christ to get ready. This was confirmed as I unpacked from my trip to Louisiana and found that I had gone back for two books on warfare he had written.

I began to focus heavily on prayer and fasting as well as intensely focus on the goals on my board. Whether they were small goals that needed to be done within a week or larger long-term goals, I made it a part of my daily life to focus and brainstorm on getting them done. After my first board was completed and I sat back and pondered on the hand of God, I decided to do another. This one would be more long-term oriented and contain several streams of income goals.

While we were in North Carolina enjoying the "pandemic," my grandfather had taken sick with Covid and was confined to a hospital. Unfortunately, he would fall ill from the very thing plaguing the earth during this time. I remember the last time we spoke to him and the last picture I sent to his phone. I don't know what made me call or send the picture, but I'm glad I did because he would remain on a ventilator for the next couple of months.

When he fell sick, I unconsciously felt as though I should be there in Louisiana. I began to question whether the move was temporary, and with time God began to reveal that it was, and it was time to plan to leave Raleigh. I knew it was His will because He took care of all of the arrangements and details regarding moving.

I hadn't really made living arrangements before going back besides putting my stuff in storage and staying at my sister's until I could get settled. My grandparent's home was still quarantined due to my grandfather still being in the hospital and them recovering from Covid. It would be a few more weeks before I could begin to get comfortable at my grandparent's home. I had recently enrolled in online classes and was ready to soar when we found out we would have to evacuate for Hurricane Laura.

This was far from the news I expected to hear at this time. I had just returned three weeks ago, and now there was a possibility of a massive natural disaster. Preparing to evacuate was a disaster in itself. My first thought was to drive back to Raleigh because "I didn't have time for this." After much persuasion, I evacuated with my family. I was extremely stressed out by the second day when it was time to leave.

I had no real plan on what I would do but knew I was determined to get back and continue with my plans.

However, I needed to get settled as soon as possible. The scenery of coming back two days after Hurricane Laura hit was like nothing I would have ever imagined. It was traumatic and very sad to see. After checking out my grandparent's home and attempting to reach others in the city by phone with no success, I decided to head to a friend's house in Baton Rouge for the night. By this time, I had a terrible headache and fell sick somewhere along the way. From there, I would drive to my ex-hubby's apartment. He had offered to let us stay and then suggested, along with everyone else, that I evacuate with the rest of the family to Dallas. Now that the storm had passed, he was open to us staying there since he was on military orders.

Days after the hurricane, we were notified that our grandfather had passed away. Things would never be the same. Not only would their home, our family home, never be the same, but we would never see him in his house again. I was beyond grateful to have given him his due honor here on earth. It was beautiful to reflect on the life and legacy of the gentle giant, my grandfather, the most consistent man in my life. I was grateful to rest in the fact that he knew my love and appreciation for him always because this would be a huge transition for our family.

Although we were living very comfortably in my ex-hubby's apartment, I was eager to get away as soon as possible. I didn't want him thinking anything or getting any ideas. My kids and I were blessed to stay at his apartment while nearly everyone affected by the storm struggled to find temporary housing and other daily provisions.

Chapter 6

Rebellion

After several weeks of living comfortably at my ex-husband's apartment while he was away, the utilities were finally back on throughout the city back home. I couldn't wait to get to my sister's house. I knew I still wouldn't be comfortable, but I had to do something. I was still determined as I had been before the storm to get my life back on track. The first step would be getting a job. Before leaving Raleigh, I reached out to a previous employer who accepted the idea of hiring me in the near future. Now that a major hurricane had just occurred, everything would be pushed back and on halt for months or even longer. While I waited on the call, I would do what I do very well, plan and grind!

I always admired myself for the ability to press through adversity and accomplish whatever I set out to accomplish. I have found myself starting over from nothing often and always came back better and with more. I was not intimidated by what I saw. On the contrary, I was anxious and determined. Although God wanted to use this time for His will, I was eager to do my own thing and on my own time and terms. That same determination shares a fine line with rebellion and pride. We can become so determined that we get out of the will of God to get to where He was going to get us anyway, His own way.

I considered returning to Monroe, so my kids could be more comfortable when I got the phone call that schools would be reopening. That was the call I had been waiting on that would calm my spirit. The kids had already been out of school since March. So, I rested in the fact that at least my son could be in school while I figured things out. This same day an older friend, who I always considered a bestie, opened the invitation to stay at his family's home if needed. I didn't consider it but would in the days to come.

One night I would finally go hang out at his house. I had been on a 21-day fast from meat and was not drinking, and of course, there were questions about it. It had been a while since I had been there, and I noticed new faces in the room. My older friend's place was known for partying, but I was used to it. It usually was me, him, his wife, his son, and maybe one other person. This time there was a guy there who seemingly loved zydeco. So, in the house tradition, they pumped me up to dance with him. It was fun, sweet, and something I had never done before. Then, he started a conversation with me in the other room and asked for my number. Now, I began to wonder if this was my husband.

Within the next couple of weeks, I had moved into my elder friend's den with my kids and was dating this person I had just met and barely knew anything about. When my male friend realized something was happening, we were on the phone, and I confessed that I was now in a relationship. We had never stopped talking, and he knew something had changed in my behavior. I was still holding on to so many things he did that were his way and not mine that I had decided I was ready to be in a relationship, and I was moving on. All he could do was accept it as he always said he would.

It turns out that the stranger I started dating was a really good guy. I would learn over the weeks and months that I was presented with this situation to learn, see, and conquer it. This was for others as well as myself. It also turned out that my elder friend whose home I was staying at was a bit more than the person I always thought he was. I saw another side of this bestie of mine but overall learned the true meaning of love covers a multitude of sins. I also learned that my life was a constant battlefield and being tried and tested through people and situations. I would soon start working two jobs in an attempt to get my own place as quickly as possible.

I didn't ask too many questions, or maybe not the right ones, but I would soon learn about the link between my elder friend and my new boyfriend, and the trauma bond and addictions related to their situation. What began to unfold were situations and demons I had never experienced so clearly and closely. My understanding was unlocking, and God equipped me to war higher in the spirit.

After a month and a half, I finally had a deposit ready for a new place. I had been proclaiming that what was for me would be on the market whenever I got my deposit. It had only been two months since the storm, and the cost of living had increased significantly. Housing was extremely limited due to demand and the number of damages throughout the area. The Holy Spirit told me to Google the management companies and check out their website. I found something that looked like perfect pricing and out of city limits. I knew it had to be for me when I went to see it. It met all of my criteria; affordable, yard, washer, and dryer. It was perfect, and it was mine.

When I began to tell others about the place, some of them encouraged me to stay closer to the city, but this offer was too good to be true right now, and I knew I couldn't let it pass me by. I was still dating, and by this time, it was clear he had a drinking problem that led to a drug problem, all rooted in childhood trauma and wounds inflicted by his parents and others. It was incredible to me to be 31 and not know the signs of these types of addictions. After several mood swings, incidents, and toxic events, I concluded that it was a regular occurrence. The long-suffering person in me wanted to see past the ugly truth.

I remember the moment I had enough and decided I would not leave empty-handed. From that moment, I was only interested in what he could do for me. I still cared, but I did not care to hear the same sob stories or deal with demons in my home. He had already been helping me financially for months, and we had grown very much as friends, but I knew this could not be my life. So, I continued to accept gifts and help and let him come around and help him whenever needed. This is when I began to see those stubborn spirits such as unforgiveness, rebellion, and pride in me that were still operating and riding on unhealed wounds.

Somewhere in the midst of this person still thinking he had a chance, my old friend reached out to me. We had kept up somewhat over the months, but I was convinced I was totally over him and had moved on with my life. I heard that he had been dealing with some girl and thought nothing of it but wished him well. We decided to meet and catch up, and everything changed when I looked at his face. It was like I fell back to earth. What had I been doing? I am still in love with this man. I couldn't believe what I was feeling. I had wasted months of my life proclaiming to be moving on while my mind and body did, but my heart was still with this person. The door had not been completely closed and the soul tie had not been severed. Instead, an additional soul tie had now been formed.

This would be the third year of trying to figure out if this was truly love, and now I was convinced. It had to be. I ended up spending more time with this person, and we continued our friendship with no sex attached. I had been celibate since realizing I had given my body over to an entire new soul tie based on my failure to accept that this person had wisdom in how he handled our situation. However, I was so stubborn and determined to have my way that I accepted the first chance offered to me and had to find out that the grass was not greener on the other side.

The emotional and mental things that I encountered during my short relationship with this new person changed me forever. The things that I learned about myself have made me better forever. I had to actually walk through these things to know for sure what is the will of the Father for my life and also to see deeper areas that I still need deliverance in. I do not doubt that God knew I would rebel and take things into my own hands, and He still worked everything out for the good once I repented and turned back to him. He used that season of my life to develop me spiritually and mentally and he also taught me how to treat His children and to stick to His script. Anything outside of that is a waste of time but God being God will turn that into a lesson learned. I decided to just let things be and focus on my goals and ministry for the time being.

Chapter 7

Healing

I had recently started working at the job I was waiting on and was accepted to another level of Sophia Ruffin's mentorship program. I was beyond excited to meet everyone in Chicago for the first time. The way that God had used this lady to minister to me and shift me for the last couple of years was apparent and I knew that it was God's will for me to be connected to her ministry. Everything about the meeting seemed to be orchestrated by God, from the seating to the groups to everything that occurred. This would be the beginning of the days of what God promised in my life.

I attended the meeting in March, was a bridesmaid for the first time in May, went to San Diego in May, and returned to Chicago in June. I attended Next Level Conference in Houston, a Prophetic Prayer conference in Birmingham, and Millions Conference in Tampa, followed by After This Glory CBK Conference back in Chicago. 2020 prepared me for all the flights and traveling I would do in 2021. It felt amazing and liberating. The only struggle would be making sure proper arrangements were made for my kids while I was gone.

After attending my dad's fifth anniversary of death events in San Diego, my ex-husband called me. A few months prior, he had a situation that opened the door for me to minister to him and point him in the right direction. All of this led to him not deploying and led to the current phone call.

He asked if I would be okay with him coming to visit and spend time with his daughter while he figured out what he would do next. This had been the first time in three years we had even held this type of cordial conversation or had much to say to each other. I thought it would be good for my kids to see us get along, and it was the right thing to do because he let us stay at his home after the hurricane. Plus, I could definitely use the help with my kids. Within a few weeks, he had made himself comfortable while staying out of my way.

We began to get more comfortable at some point, and the four of us started to do things together. I began to question whether it was God's will for me to be married and opened up to the idea that God could repair our damaged and at this point, hardly existent relationship. I was considering that this had to be what this meant. With all the good things God is showing me, this must be a part of it.

This was an important trip for me since we had been praying as a team for my Coach's mother. I was hoping that everything would go smoothly so I could complete my current assignment as an intercessor and receive the proper impartation necessary for the journey ahead. During this trip, I shared with a teammate things God had told me concerning my ex-husband and me, things I would later regret sharing because of the level of accountability necessary. However, all went well, and when I returned, my ex-hubby insisted on taking us to a beach for a mini-vacation on the way home. In the back of my mind, I knew he was still toxic, but somewhere I wanted to believe that God chose Him and wanted to restore things.

After a couple of months of arguments and throwback conversations, I concluded that this person and their baggage needed to leave my space. I could not tolerate such bold demons. My home was just not big enough. I continued to do what I had been doing but wondered when God would send my person into my life. I believed God but somewhat questioned His way of doing things. Nevertheless, I maintained my focus and kept pressing toward the goals before me.

I spent the remainder of 2021 working on myself, my brand, and focusing on my goals. Finally, God began to deal with me about making a move. The revelations were continuous, and I knew it was His will, but He began to instruct me in wisdom. He began to show me that there were assignments that needed to be completed and doors that needed to be closed before I could walk into this next season. He gave me the word "due season" during this time. I didn't know then, but this would be the word of the Lord concerning my life and lives of others for 2022.

I would spend the Christmas and New Year holidays torn between if it was God's will for me to restore a dead relationship or if there was something new, He wanted to do through me. God began to deal with me heavily through Apostle Eckhardt about doublemindedness. I began to seek knowledge on this stronghold and realized I needed to get free from it. Although I realized there were things I could have done differently in marriage, the fact was I was mentally and emotionally abused. No matter how much I changed myself, that person mainly remained the same. The doublemindedness I was walking in resulted from the soul ties I had made with different people over the years, and the main one was a covenant that was made before God when I married this person.

When I finally began to accept that things could have been different, but they are what they are, and ultimately what we make them, I began to forgive myself and release myself from the soul tie and covenant I had made with every single person. I have done this over the years, but I was renouncing from a place of knowledge and understanding this time. I began to learn about ungodly covenants and dismantling ungodly altars. I began to understand the weaknesses in my flesh that were targeted to get me out of covenant and out of the will of God time and time again. When I came to the knowledge of a "covenant-breaking spirit," I began to see how the enemy had been working diligently to derail my life.

I can look back and see how the rejection, trauma, rebellion, lust, and sin led up to this moment. I was no longer willing to accept what life gave me and wanted what God had for me. I decided to be free from double-mindedness and make up my mind about what I wanted to do, be, and have in life and that is what God says I shall do, be, and have. I decided to walk boldly as a daughter of the King and believe what God was showing me about my future. I would no longer take things into my own hands but would wait on God and His timing for my life. When I made this decision, I began to walk in a supernatural level of peace and joy. Whatever God has in store in 2022, I believe I will not only be a recipient but will testify of His miracles, signs, and wonders and refer to these things as a reminder.

> [8] *"For my thoughts are not your thoughts,*
> *neither are your ways my ways,"*
> *declares the* LORD.

Shameka Oliver

> [9] *"As the heavens are higher than the earth,*
> *so are my ways higher than your ways*
> *and my thoughts than your thoughts.*
> **Isaiah 55:8-9**

Following the *After This Glory Conference*, my coach shifted the program, and we were promoted to the *Company of Copacetic Leaders*. God revealed to me how we had crossed over at the conference as leaders and that what He was doing through our Coach and us had already been established in all the earth. He began to take me through a series of lessons to stretch and grow my faith and character. He began to supernaturally highlight me and open doors of favor and opportunities. Holy Spirit began to prompt me to host prayer challenges on social media. I began to engage more and grow my content on my platforms. He began to show me how He was setting things in order behind the scene, and all I had to do was be ready to shift when He said so. All in all, He was perfecting my obedience to Him and ability to hear His voice. He was preparing me for the promise.

CHAPTER 8

Freedom

The word of the Lord to me for 2022 was Due Season. "You shall not make idols for yourselves or erect an image or pillar, and you shall not set up a figured stone in your land to bow down to it, for I am the LORD your God. **2** You shall keep my Sabbaths and reverence my sanctuary: I am the LORD.

3 "If you walk in my statutes and observe my commandments and do them, **4** then I will give you your rains in their season, and the land shall yield its increase, and the trees of the field shall yield their fruit. **5** Your threshing shall last to the time of the grape harvest, and the grape harvest shall last to the time for sowing. And you shall eat your bread to the full and dwell in your land securely. **6** I will give peace in the land, and you shall lie down, and none shall make you afraid. And I will remove harmful beasts from the land, and the sword shall not go through your land. **7** You shall chase your enemies, and they shall fall before you by the sword. **8** Five of you shall chase a hundred, and a hundred of you shall chase ten thousand, and your enemies shall fall before you by the sword. **9** I will turn to you and make you fruitful and multiply you and will confirm my covenant with you. **10** You shall eat old store long kept, and you shall clear out the old to make way for the new. **11** I will make my dwelling among you, and my soul shall not abhor you. **12** And I will walk among you and will be your God, and you shall be my people. **13** I am the LORD your God, who brought you out of the land of Egypt, that you should not be their slaves. And I have broken the bars of your yoke and made you walk erect (Leviticus 26).

I hadn't realized when I released this word in November that this would be the word for 2022, but what He revealed on January 1, 2022, further confirmed it through another scripture:

"The land you are entering to take up ownership isn't like Egypt, the land you left, where you had to plant your own seed and water it yourselves as in a vegetable garden. But the land you are about to cross the river and take for your own is a land of mountains and valleys; it drinks water that rains from the sky. It's a land that God, your God, personally tends—he's the gardener—he alone keeps his eye on it all year long" (Deuteronomy 11:10-12 MSG).

When I received these words from the Lord, my faith began to stir uncontrollably. I began to walk boldly and without fear of the future, knowing I was pressing towards a mark with a purpose and expected end ahead. The enemy started to send attacks to distract me, but I could discern the lesson and keep it moving in power and authority. I began to let the Holy Spirit have His way and be at peace with the timing of the Lord. As I began to wait on the Lord and trust in His promise completely, I began to see the answers to prayers manifest all around me. As I began to gain more understanding and knowledge about ungodly soul ties, covenants, and coming out of agreement with them, I began to see myself break through a glass ceiling. It was as if another level of life had been unlocked for me. I started to walk in the manifestation of freedom in Christ.

The Holy Spirit revealed to me the cycles of dysfunction that began when my great-grandmother had my grandmother out of wedlock. She had recently been widowed and never married my grandmother's dad who was a "white" or creole man. My great grandmother was a much darker skinned lady. I don't know what the details were of their relationship, but I do know it began a cycle that would be repeated for generations. The Holy Spirit revealed to me how my grandmother and her mother were rejected because of the color of their skin. In those days "white" or creole people were very hateful towards those of darker skin tones.

My grandmother went through her life without her father and went on to bare the children of three "creole" men and relive the same situation as her mother. Rejection for not being light enough from the first two and whatever the details were that led to the abandonment by the third. This was then passed down to my mother, who would go on to choose different types of men, but the demonic cycle of rejection and abandonment would continue.

It took for me to live through many years of wounding myself over and over again and trying to be my own god, failing and getting back up, repeating the same cycles over and over before I realized that there were demonic covenants that needed to be severed that were made knowingly, unknowingly, and generations ago. This knowledge has changed the trajectory of my life and my legacy forever.

I have genuinely learned on my journey that God is who He says He is and He will do what He said He would do. There has never been a time on my journey when God did not keep His promises to me. Since I was a little girl, He has always made Himself known and watched over His word to perform it. Even when I went my own way, He would lovingly lead me back to His perfect will. He knew that at the set time, DUE SEASON, that I would stumble across the knowledge of the deliverance that was the key to my next level.

Since being delivered from double-mindedness and completely dismantling and severing ungodly soul ties and covenant and demonic altars, I began to see my prayers being answered at an accelerated rate. This would be the year I turn 33, and God had been telling me triple, triple, double, double. I began to see the manifestation of this as fast as I began to declare it. The people I am assigned to pray for in my life started to receive miracles and wonders. As God dealt with me on the prayer challenges, my life became more disciplined almost immediately. I made changes in my diet, budget, and household. **The year 2022 had been declared a year of restoration and me, and my family were beginning to reap the manifestations of that declaration.**

As I was focusing on the goals ahead of me and pursuing purpose, things were working in my favor. I missed our first quarterly team meeting with The Company of Copacetic Leaders, but I was completely engaged via the live stream. It was so powerful and so clear that our Coach had shifted and now had to take us to another level. The pour was so anointed that it was tangible even through Zoom. Every time my coach spoke, I knew I was assigned to her life and ministry. The meeting shifted and awakened something in me that I hadn't realized was still asleep.

When I scheduled the meeting with my coach, I was excited to have a conversation because I had missed the meeting and we hadn't all gathered since the September conference. She had recently announced that she would be in Houston, and I knew I would definitely attend. As our call began, I began to ask her how she was and didn't know she would be in Houston soon. The conversation continued when she said that the Lord said I would serve her while she was there. I almost shed tears as I expressed to her how the Lord had revealed to me that I was assigned to her ministry and how blessed I had been because of it.

Not only had I been fasting regularly, but this was on the first day of my monthly fast and the second day of my very first prayer challenge. I share that to say that obedience and surrender has been the key to the favor God has allowed me to walk in and is getting ready to walk me into. He was demonstrating to me that what I was doing in secret was being rewarded in the open. I kept my hand to the plow in spite of the adversity that tried to distract me during this time.

Whenever the enemy comes to whisper his lies about why I shouldn't be doing what I am doing or why I should doubt God or not be obedient, I shut him down with a loud act of obedience. Whether that is a social media prayer challenge, doing a Facebook Live, writing a book, or making a lifestyle change, I am determined to ensure that I continually seek the Lord's will and not my own will. I believe everything He has declared through His prophets for the year 2022, and I want to ensure that I am on the right side of this DUE SEASON.

Triple, triple, double, double for me is manifesting as answered prayer for myself and those around me, open doors, new doors, new revelations, new ideas, favor, peace, grace, financial increase, **triumph, and restoration. The Lord said that there would be a reaping of what was sown in this due season. This will** be the time that was prophesied. While the world may be in chaos, the kingdom of God is being manifested on earth through the sons and daughters of God. I am filled with peace and joy at the revelation that God has carried me through the years and kept me all the way to the point of my DUE SEASON, where the curse that had been haunting my bloodline is broken for good. I am ready to receive everything God has ordained for me from the foundation of the Earth. I receive everything the enemy has stolen from my bloodline for generations triple, triple, double, double in Jesus' name.

To any person, young or old, who has struggled with sin, trauma, identity crisis, shame, or dysfunctional and toxic cycles, be encouraged today in knowing that God is a deliverer. Although we sometimes get out of alignment with His perfect will for our lives, He is faithful and just to forgive us and redeem us. Sometimes we don't know or understand that we are inflicting ourselves with wounds and attaching ourselves to others, thinking that temporary feeling is healing. I hope that my story blesses you and helps you break free from any soul ties that have you bound and have been hindering you from walking in the fullness of who God created you to be and hindering you from walking in His divine purpose for your life. I want to encourage you to never give up on God and the vision He has placed inside you for your life. Take the time to examine yourself and your life and seek knowledge about your personal situation. Seek leaders who have visible fruit of the spirit who can help by counseling or walking alongside you on your journey of deliverance and keeping you accountable. Trust the process and endure until you see the manifestation of the promises that God showed you.

"Yes indeed, it won't be long now." God's Decree. "Things are going to happen so fast your head will swim, one thing fast on the heels of the other. You won't be able to keep up. Everything will be happening at once—and everywhere you look, blessings! Blessings like wine pouring off the mountains and hills. I'll make everything right again for my people Israel: "They'll rebuild their ruined cities. They'll plant vineyards and drink good wine. They'll work their gardens and eat fresh vegetables. And I'll plant them, plant them on their own land. They'll never again be uprooted from the land I've given them." God, your God, says so" (Amos 9:13-15 MSG).

PRAYER

Father God, in the name of Jesus, we come to you this day thanking you for sending your son Christ Jesus to die on the cross for us so that we may have redemption of sin and be reconciled to you. We thank you that He also died and that every curse may be broken off our lives by His blood. We thank you for this precious sacrifice of love, God, and we use the authority you have given us by the blood of the Lamb. We sever any ungodly soul ties and covenants we have made with people, whether knowingly or unknowingly through sex or any other type of intimate relationship that was not in order in your sight. By the power of the blood, we dismantle any demonic altars that have been established in our lives or over our bloodlines. We go back five, six, and seven generations and plead the blood of Jesus on any established demonic altar that affects us today. We come out of agreement with any curse spoken by any person, whether jokingly or out of hatred or anger, and dismantle the assignments of hell over our bloodline. We ask that you give us the knowledge and understanding to walk in freedom, power, and strength to go back for those who are still bound. We thank you that who the son sets free is free indeed, and as we begin to walk in freedom, we will begin to see the perfect will of the father manifest in our lives on earth as it is in heaven in Jesus' name. Amen.

www.ingramcontent.com/pod-product-compliance
Lightning Source LLC
Chambersburg PA
CBHW051700090426
42736CB00013B/2466